HOLIDAY SCRAPBOOK PAPER PIZAZZ™!

BETTERWAY BOOKS

Cincinnati, Ohio

01   00   99   5   4   3

ISBN 1-55870-478-7

Album page designer: Bridgette Server

Finally you can take your precious photos out of those shoe boxes and place them in albums to be shared with family and friends. This new craft called memory albums or scrapbooking is very easy to do. Just as in kindergarten, all you do is cut and paste! It's critical to use acid-free products so your photos do not deteriorate any faster than nature allows. We like to slip the finished pages into sheet protectors (acid-free and PVC free, of course) then into a 3-ring binder. This way it's easy to add pages or re-arrange them. Don't make creating your album pages a chore. Do a few pages at a sitting, using the ideas in Paper Pizazz™ books to save time. Begin with your most recent photos and work back in time. Most of all, relax, have fun and enjoy creating your pages.

BASIC SUPPLIES:

- Fiskars® straight-edged scissors
- Fiskars® Paper Edgers scissors
- ruler
- black permanent ink pen
- acid-free adhesive

1 Sort your photos by date, then by theme. Whether it's one prized photo on a page or 3–6 photos, it helps to have a common thread connecting the photos. Set your photos on the page and decide which work best together.

2 Cut your photos to keep only the most important parts. This is called cropping. Be sure to save historical features like a house, car or piece of furniture— they'll be fun to see ten years from now. It's best to keep the scissors in one position and move the photo as you cut around the images. You can also crop in shapes like stars, hearts, etc. For perfect circles and ovals, use plastic stencils. See the page ideas in this book for more ideas.

3 Select your papers. One patterned sheet can be the background page. Another simpler pattern or a plain sheet can be cut as a frame or mat around your cropped photo. First glue the photo to the selected sheet. Then cut the paper ¼"–½" away from the photo. For another effect, double-mat some photos.

4 Arrange your photos on the background sheet until you like the placement. Use images from the cutouts page of this book to add decorative touches. Glue the pieces in place.

5 Journaling may be the most important step. While many people don't like their handwriting, it adds a valuable personal touch. Name, date and place are helpful to write, but it's important to give more information. "Grandma, June 1996 in her flower garden" is good but "June 1996—Grandma is very proud of her flower garden. She won ribbons every year at the county fair. Grandma taught all six grandchildren the wonder of growing things" is better. Write on a plain colored sheet, then cut it out, or write directly on the background sheet.

BIRTHDAY THEMES

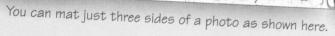

You can mat just three sides of a photo as shown here.

Ryan's 11th birthday. Uncle Bob gave him a fishing pole and tackle box, then took him fishing. He caught one within 10 minutes!

"It sure is fun bein' one!"
Brianna
Feb. 6, 1995

Many of the Paper Pizazz™ sheets are effective when cut into strips and used as decorative elements.

A birthday countdown beginning with 76-year-old grandpa.

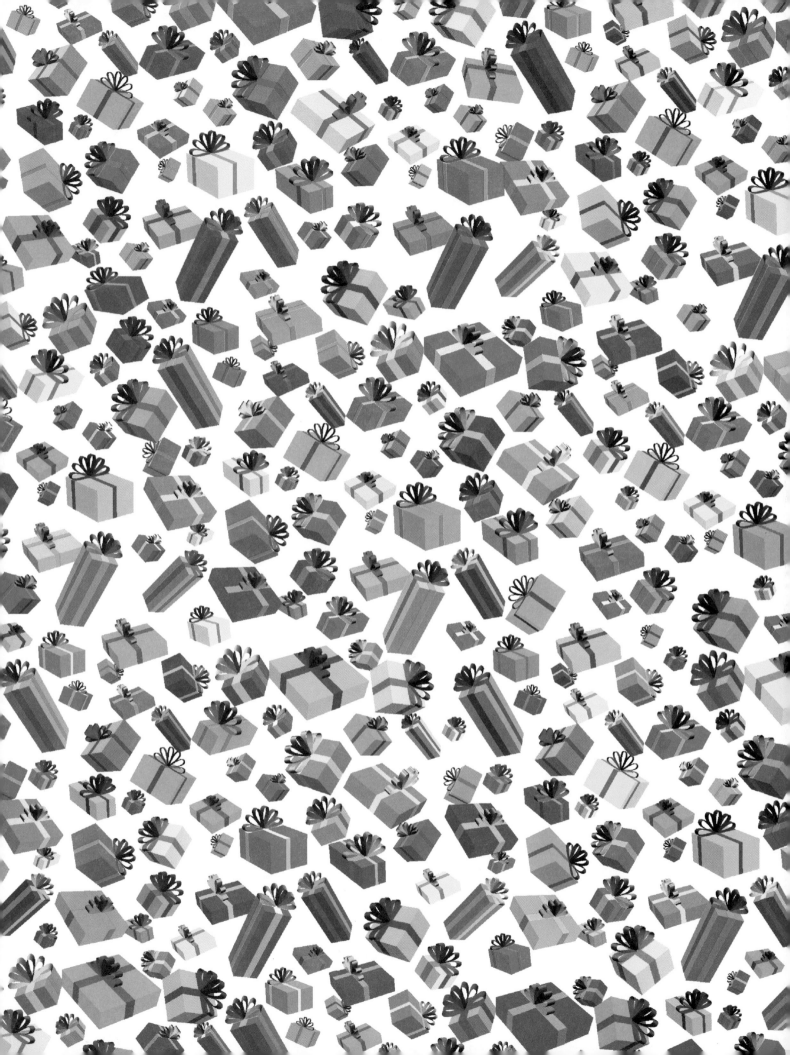

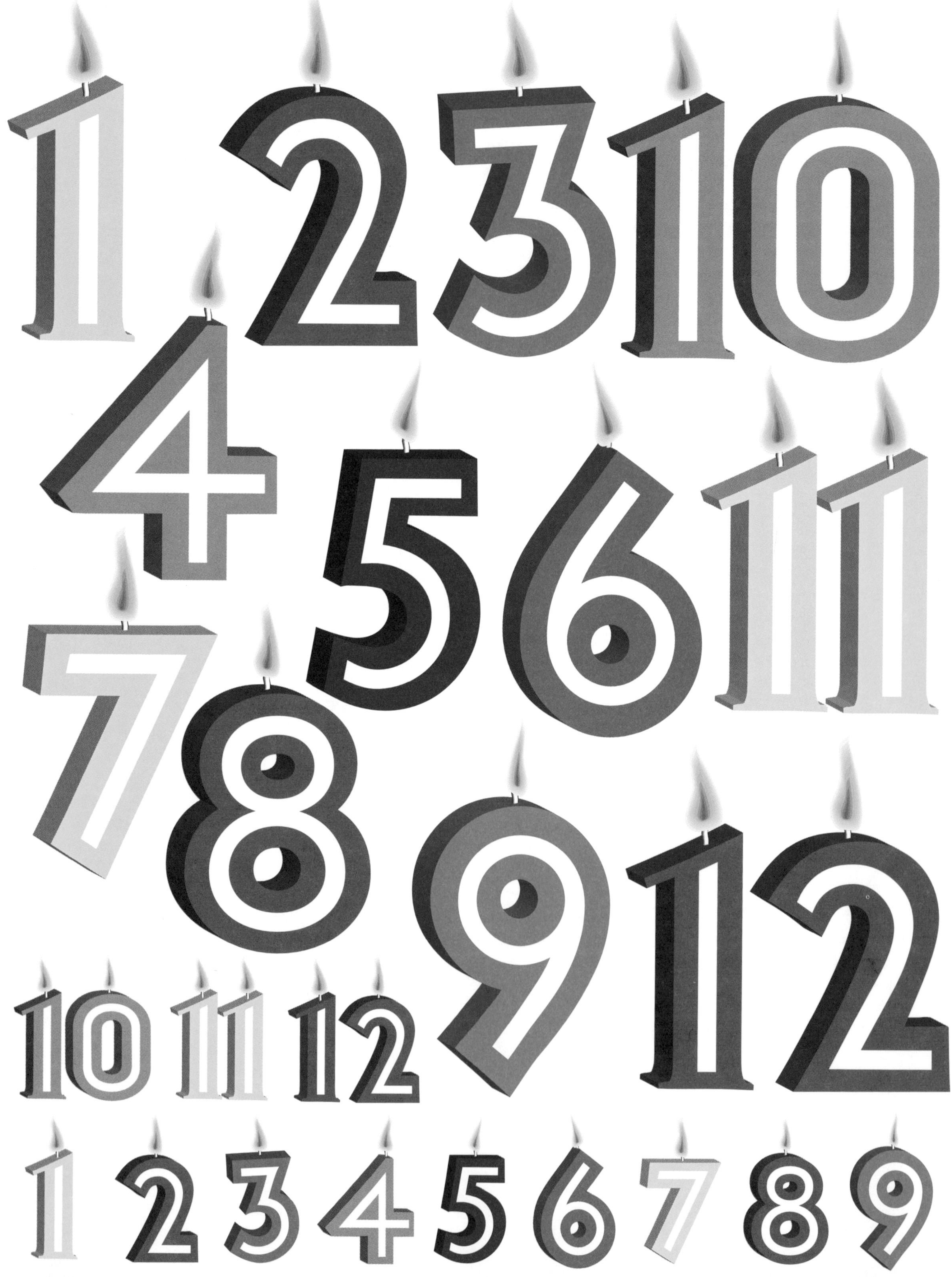

Happy Birthday

HAPPY BIRTHDAY

CHRISTMAS THEMES

Christmas 1988
Joey & Elsa talk to Santa
The lists get longer … and longer … and longer …

"Just What I Wanted!"
Elsa opening her gift on Christmas, 1989

The gift wrapped page would be effective with Paper Pizazz™ Birthday papers, too.

Christmas 1986

Jasper checks out the forest smells on the tree

HO HO HO

new ornaments for this year

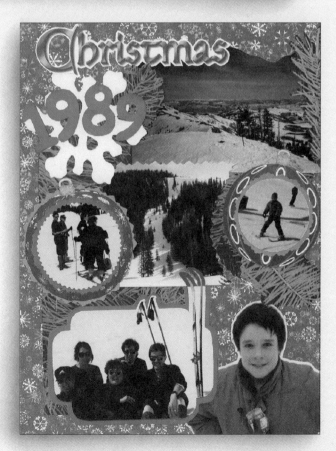

Christmas 1989

Notice how pieces of the pine paper are cut out and attached around the photos.

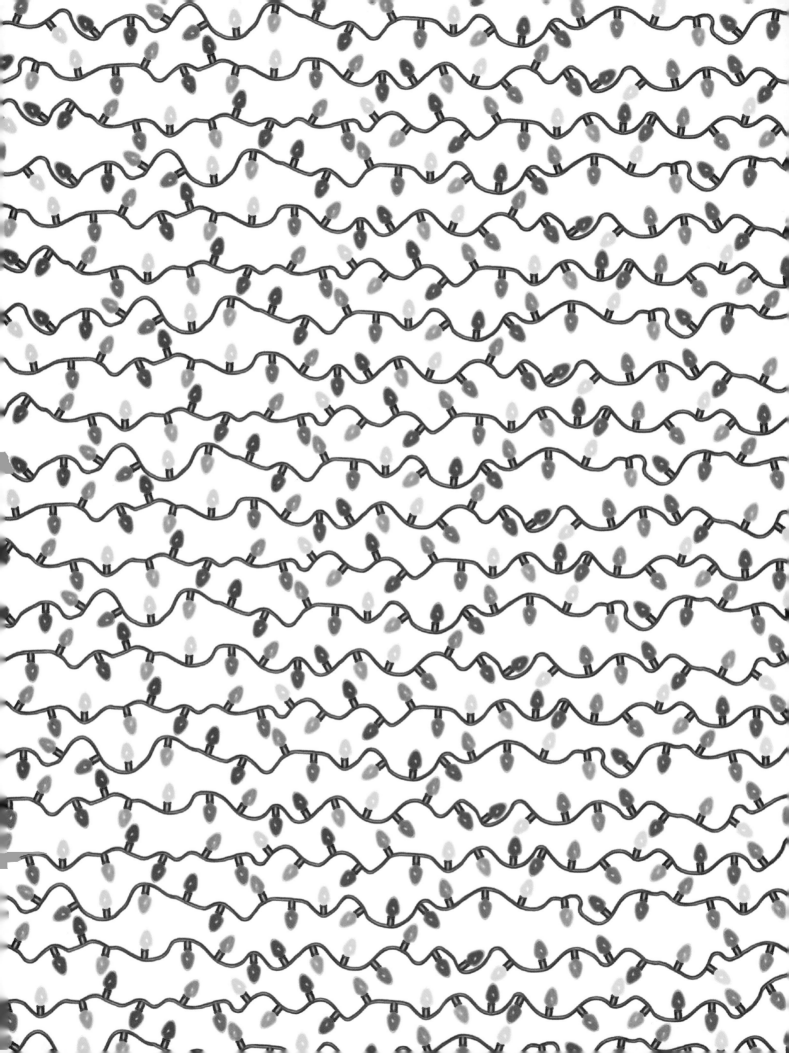

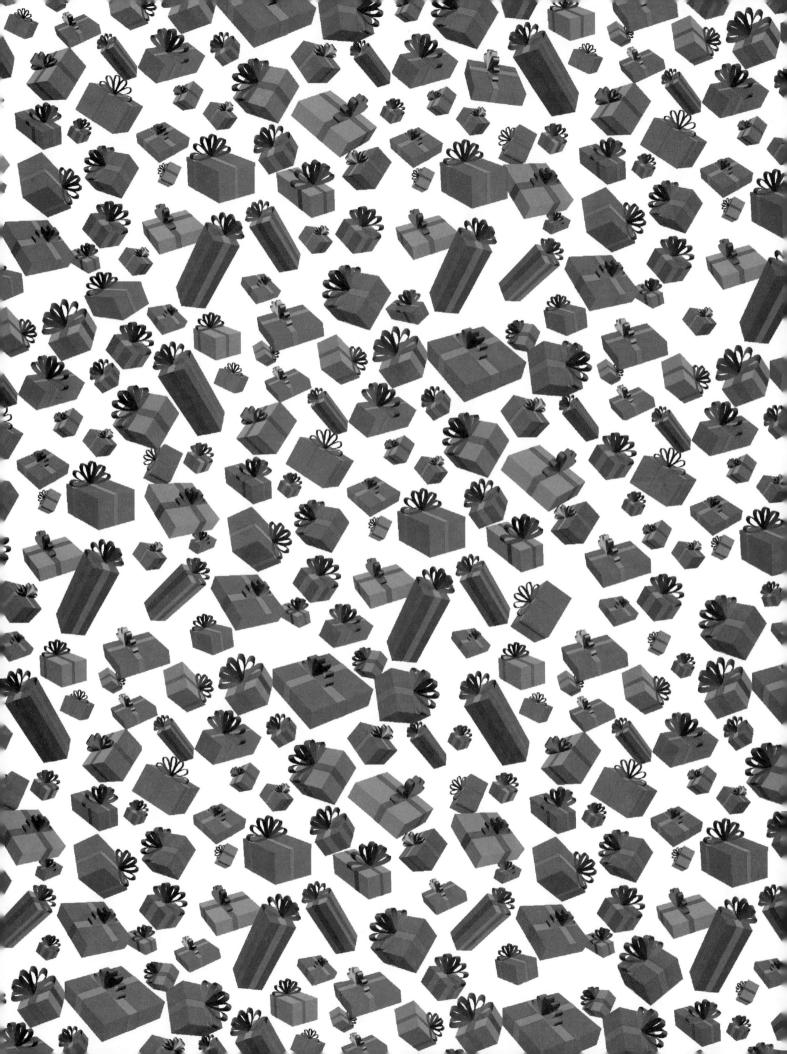

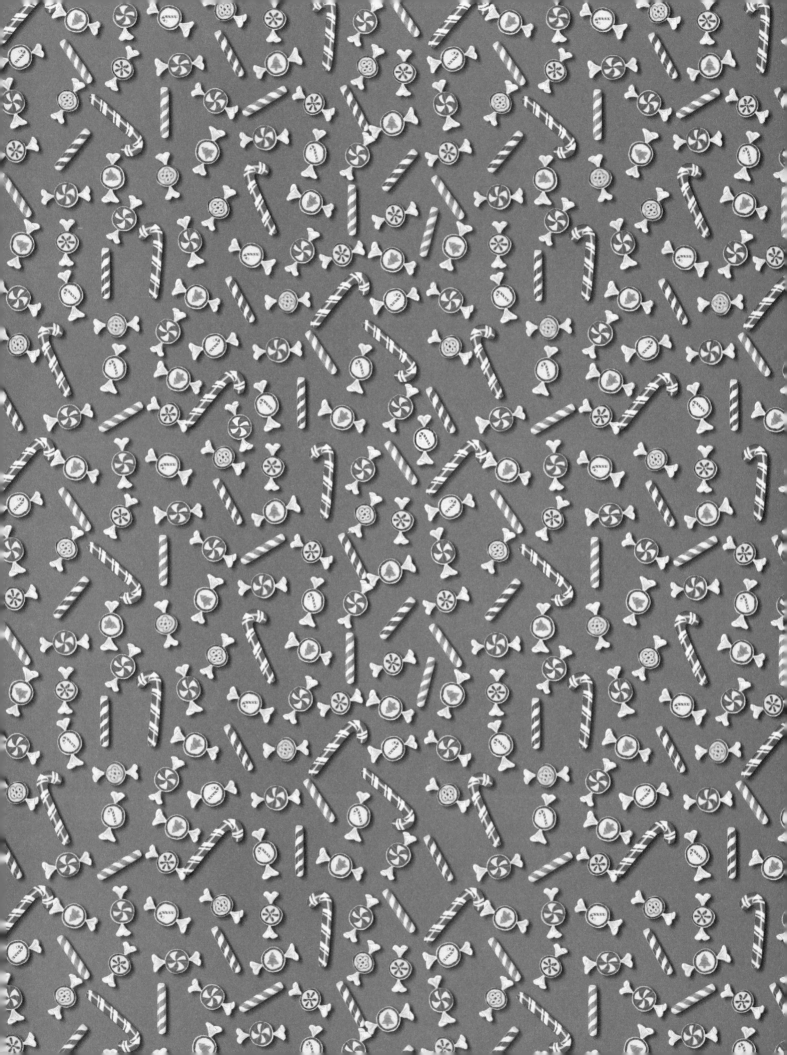

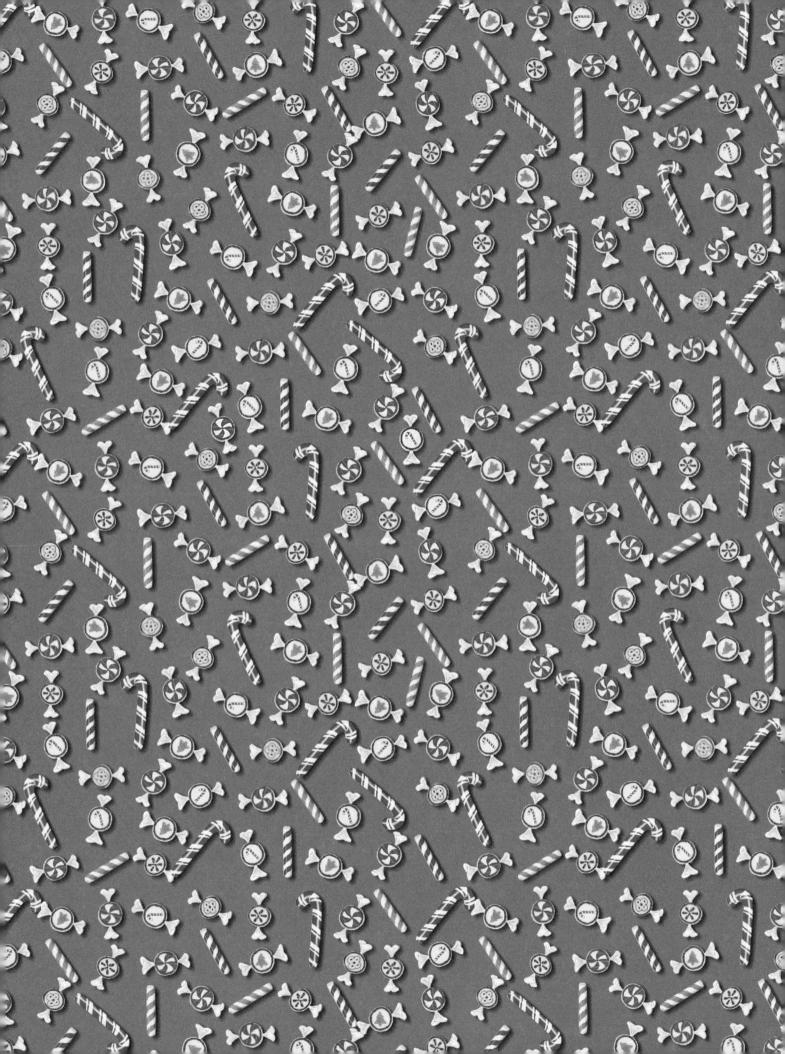

HOLIDAYS
AND SEASONS
THEMES

JULY 4
1993

~MENU~
HOT DOGS
BURGERS
POTATO SALAD
COLE SLAW
JELLO MOLD
CORN ON THE COB

ICE CREAM
BROWNIES
WATERMELLON

SODA POP

BEER

Mother's Day
1996

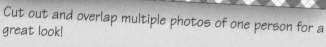

Cut out and overlap multiple photos of one person for a great look!

BEST FRIEND VALENTINES

Spooks & Spoons
Halloween 1994

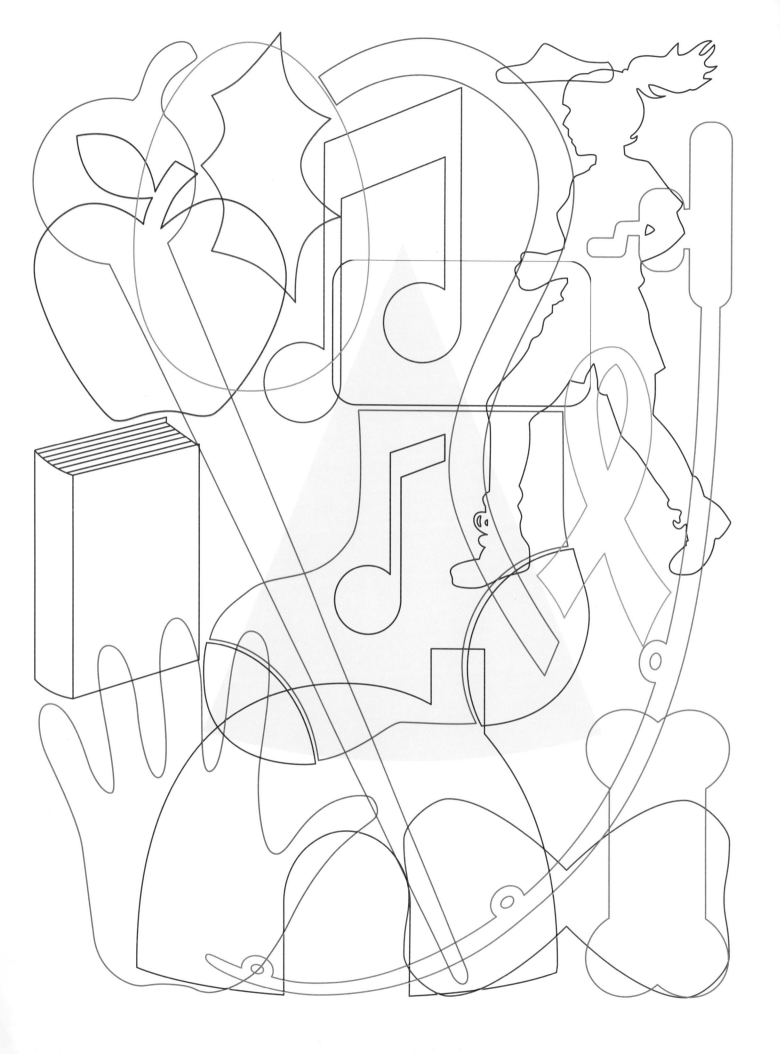

Use these lettering styles as a guide for your album pages.

BLOCK LETTERING

BUBBLE LETTERING

BALL & STICK LETTERING